WELcome!

We're so happy you picked up this book. We're always excited to meet people who want to use their creativity to make the world a better place!

Anyone can change the world. It's fun, you can learn a ton, and it doesn't need to be overwhelming. Change already happens all around us—seasons change, feelings change, *we* change. It's all good. We all take part in creating our world. Each of us has a place, no matter what our background, skin color, economic status, or political philosophy. And the best part? When enough people realize they can be the change, our whole world can change, and for the better.

"If you don't like something, change it.
If you can't change it, change your attitude."
-Maya Angelou

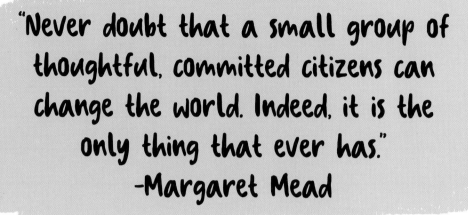

> "Never doubt that a small group of thoughtful, committed citizens can change the world. Indeed, it is the only thing that ever has."
> —Margaret Mead

Being the change is a creative act. We create all the time through what we say and think, what we wear, and the actions we take. We do it through music, art, science, relationships, sports, you name it. Any time you mix your imagination with expression, you get creativity.

To create is to make something out of nothing. To be creative, you just need a little imagination. Author Amy Whitaker, an expert in creativity, calls this "inventing point B." As we imagine and work toward our goal step by step, we get from point A to point B. It's that simple.

Creative ideas are all around you, waiting to be discovered! You can turn ideas into reality using your talents, skills, energy, and time. You can even tap into your friends' talents and skills. Creative ideas happen when you connect the dots between ideas that normally don't go together to come up with something amazing and totally new. They can range from imagining a more beautiful world to innovating a way to get computers to kids who don't have them.

As the sister-team behind Hello!Lucky, we love the visual arts for expressing creativity because it's a universal form of communication. No matter what language you speak,

you can understand pictures (true fact!). Pictures can instantly connect you to others who share your vision and speed up the time it takes to make it a reality.

You might be thinking, "But I'm not creative!" That's definitely not true. No matter who you are, **you can strengthen your creative powers through practice.** A lot of times, creativity is made synonymous with artistic talent. But creativity is so much more than just being good at art.

You can connect creative ideas by daydreaming. (During school might not be the best time. Trust us, the info you learn at school will give you raw material for your creative ideas!) **Be curious and look around for inspiration.** Take in the world, talk about what you observe with friends, and then express it by writing, doodling, or even doing the projects in this book. With time, you'll be able to tap into your creative power and make positive changes in ways you couldn't even imagine!

So let's get started. No matter where you begin, or how big or small a starting point you choose, you can use your creativity to be the change! The future is in your hands, and we're excited to see what you create.

Be powerful. Be kind. Inspire and be inspired. Work alone or together. Keep going. And most importantly, have fun!

XOXO
EUNICE AND
SABRINA

"If you can dream it,
you can do it."
-Walt Disney

OUR STORY

As sisters, we grew up living in countries radically different from our own, all over the world. We marveled at how people create happy and fulfilling lives in conditions ranging from extreme poverty to extreme wealth. As filmmaker Yann Arthus-Bertrand observes in his documentary *Human*, whether the glass is half empty or half full, it's a beautiful glass.

After we started our company, Hello!Lucky, in 2003, we learned several important lessons that helped inspire us to write this book.

1 If you can dream it, you can create it.

When we were kids, we had no idea that someday we'd be able to work together doing what we love, having fun, and giving back to our community. That said, we also didn't believe that it was *not* possible. Our parents encouraged us to be pragmatic while following our passions. Step by step, we built our company, and today we are still imagining the future and taking the next steps to make it happen.

Small actions can make a big difference.

In 2015, our friends at Egg Press had the simple idea to challenge ourselves and our friends to write 30 letters in 30 days during April, National Letter Writing Month. We posted the challenge and got an amazing response! The Write_On Campaign now has over 10,000 members. This amazing community helped to inspire our book *Happy Mail*.

3 When you speak out with a clear, positive vision, people listen.

In 2015, Sabrina realized that products like our greeting cards can help people connect to positive values such as creativity, human connection, and fair labor standards. She decided it should be easier for small creative businesses to sell their goods internationally. She expressed her views at a local meeting for small businesses, and through a series of surprising connections, she was invited to become a small businesses trade advocate—and to have dinner with President and First Lady Obama at the White House! Sometimes, when you articulate a positive vision based on personal experience, like-minded people—and people in power—pay attention.

4 Creativity can unify people and give them a voice.

Any time you gather a group of people to make change, there are bound to be differences that slow you down. This is known as the "collective action problem," a.k.a. herding cats. That's where creativity comes in. Powerful images and words can help people clarify what they collectively want and take decisive action.

We believe that creativity is a powerful tool for political good—for fairness, respect, and inclusion of everyone. After the 2016 U.S. presidential election, we created *The Future is in Your Hands* campaign, which used fun T-shirts, totes, and mugs to inspire people to vote. We created posters for the Women's March on Washington, which were downloaded over 2,000 times, and designed enamel pins that have raised thousands of dollars for good causes.

We love being the change, and we hope you do too. Enjoy the journey, and watch your creativity unfold into real, positive impact!

SECTION ONE:

BE THE CHANGE

"If we could change ourselves, the tendencies in the world would also change. As a man changes his own nature, so does the attitude of the world change towards him. ...We need not wait to see what others do."
-Mahatma Gandhi

WHAT DOES IT MEAN TO BE THE CHANGE?

Put simply, Gandhi said that the power to change the world comes from within you—nowhere else. **Change in the outer world happens in direct response to changes you make in your inner world.** Whether you want to see fewer homeless animals, bigger rainforests, less government waste, or more people leading healthy, happy lives, the only person in the world that you can change is yourself.

You can start anytime you choose. No matter how challenging your circumstances, if you begin to trust in and be curious about yourself, and look for the positive in everyone, you will find the courage and clarity to move forward.

With practice, you can learn to tame your thoughts so that you consistently feel peaceful, chill, and calm. Then you can channel your positive energy into action. With a keen focus on your desires and goals, you can begin to turn your vision into reality.

Being the change naturally leads to giving back and serving others. Why? Because when you see the good in yourself, you can't help but see the good in others. We are all interconnected. When you realize this, you become someone who innately cares for others, accepts your circumstances, and knows that you are free to create your world.

Being the change doesn't mean you need to give up all material things. Everyone is here to discover their own path and purpose. For some, it might be creating useful products, wealth, and jobs by starting a successful business. For others, it might be becoming a teacher or social worker. There is no right or wrong answer. Regardless of what you choose to do, **being the change is about owning your power** to see the world and to help create it. How you decide to do it is entirely up to you.

GOOD VIBES ONLY

You may not realize it, but you have the potential to be a steady source of good vibes to the people around you—and to the entire world.

Inspirational authors Esther and Jerry Hicks teach that you are like a radio antennae, broadcasting your signals, and receiving the broadcasts of others who are tuned into the same frequency as you. **When your vibes are positive, you attract more positivity.** When your vibes are negative, you attract more negativity. Your positive attitudes, actions, and words attract positive people and opportunities, amplifying your power to create a better world.

> "Perpetual optimism is a force multiplier."
> –Colin Powell

Luckily, it's not hard to tune into your good vibes. The Hicks also suggest that we each have a natural stream of well-being inside of us. You might recognize this as the feeling you get when you do something you love. When you're connected to the stream, you feel good. When you're not, you don't. **With practice, you can learn to tune into your good vibes any time.**

Feelings are just thoughts in action. It's easy to spot negative thoughts because they make us feel bad. We can also spot positive thoughts because they make us feel like we are floating downstream. They give us a sense of relief and happiness.

Unfortunately, many of us get stuck in a pattern of negative thoughts, such as "not good enough" or "not smart enough." These thoughts are not who we truly are. Whether they come from our parents' well-intentioned criticisms or our peers' judgments of us, we can learn to question these thoughts. As speaker and author Byron Katie suggests, we can ask ourselves: Is it true? How do I feel and act when I believe this thought? Is there a more positive thought that could be more true? When you inquire into your thoughts, you tune into your inner voice and connect to your power to be the change. Thus, being the change creates a virtuous cycle.

BE THE CHANGE—VIRTUOUS CYCLE

LOVE AND RESPECT YOURSELF, AND TRUST LIFE

FEEL JOY, APPRECIATION, AND COMPASSION FOR OTHERS

CONNECT TO PEOPLE ON A SIMILAR PATH

PEOPLE AROUND YOU FEEL YOUR GOOD VIBES
AND MIRROR THEM BACK TO YOU

RECEIVE EVEN MORE ENERGY TO CREATE
THE WORLD YOU WANT TO SEE

YOUR ACTIONS MAKE RIPPLE EFFECTS
THROUGHOUT YOUR COMMUNITY, AND EVEN THE WORLD!

WHY SHOULD I BE THE CHANGE?

When you decide to be the change, you activate **a powerful core of positive energy** that radiates outward and attracts people and opportunities. As you spend more energy creating and less energy on self-criticism, doubt, guilt, or blame, you can begin to have **an even greater positive impact** on the world.

Think of Gandhi, who led the movement for Indian independence from the United Kingdom. Focused inner work and positive vision fueled his decades of effort—no challenge ever caused him to give up. His belief in *all* people's right to exist—even when they were oppressing others—enabled him to take a strong stand and engage in assertive, peaceful conflict.

Think of Rosa Parks, who helped spark the Civil Rights Movement. Rosa's influence is not because she simply refused to give up her seat on the bus that day (many had refused before her). Rosa's impact stems from her clear vision and goal for who she wanted to be.

Emma Seppala writes that research by Dr. Martin Seligman, Dr. Robert A. Emmons, and others has shown that self-compassion, gratitude, and altruism—which are essential parts of being the change—are scientifically linked to health and happiness. So the more people who decide to be the change, the happier and healthier human beings and our entire planet will become. Now that's something we're excited to see!

> "Each person must live their life as a model for others." -Rosa Parks

HOW CAN I BE THE CHANGE?

Where to start? It's up to you. You can read books, watch videos, talk to friends, or study a faith tradition—we've found that most faiths agree on basic principles like love, abundance and trust, connecting to your own inner being, and forgiveness. Just pick up a thread that inspires you and follow it. Here are a few tips to get you started:

* **Understand your feelings.** There are positive feelings and negative feelings, and each one serves a purpose. For example, anger may mean that you need to set boundaries. Learn to listen to what your feelings are telling you.

* **Look honestly at your limitations, whether internal (e.g., are you an introvert or an extrovert?) or external (e.g., from your family or environment).** Acknowledge them and meet yourself wherever you are.

* **Cultivate a growth mindset.** As psychologist Dr. Carol Dweck observes, people who see themselves as always growing through hard work can achieve more than those who see their talents as fixed. We are all constantly evolving and growing. Setbacks and successes are opportunities to learn. Keep setting your sights on your next goal, and then allow it to happen.

* **You don't need to be superhuman to be the change.** If something isn't working, take a break. The time may not be right for your idea, or you may need to approach it differently.

* **Don't try to change other people.** Remember, the only person you have the power to change is yourself. You do you. Allow other people to do what they want and be the change they want to see in the world too.

* **Embrace diverse viewpoints.** We live in a wildly beautiful, diverse world. All views add depth to what we can create together.

CHANGE A LITTLE EVERY DAY

In order to be the change, you need to make a daily habit of getting to your happy place. Some of the ways to get there include meditation, exercising, doodling, reading books, or watching TV shows or movies that inspire you and make you feel good. (Avoid dystopian books about post-apocalyptic zombie invasions! That is *so* not the change you want to see!)

Find what works for you and go for it! A little bit of change every day goes a long way.

SECTION TWO:

MAKE the CHANGE

"Imagination is everything. It is the preview
of life's coming attractions."
-Albert Einstein

> *"Creativity brings good things in the world that otherwise would not exist. It's a noble act of pushing back darkness and giving hope to despair."* -Jeff Goins

Now that you know what it means to *be* the change, let's talk about what it means to use your creativity to *make* the change!

WHAT IS CREATIVITY?

Creativity is good feelings + imagination + action. Creativity mixes together our personal experiences, stories we've heard, or things we've read about with our intuition and inspiration to create a brand-new idea.

Creativity thrives when you feel good and take focused action. This state of effortless productivity is what psychologist Mihaly Csikszentmihalyi calls "flow." You may have experienced this state of being in the zone when you were doing something you enjoy or worked hard on a project. The truth is, this state is available to you at any time!

Sometimes it's hard to get into your creative flow, and that's okay. You can just walk away for a bit and let things percolate. Often, our best ideas come to us when we're thinking about something else!

CREATIVE WAYS TO MAKE CHANGE

Creativity starts with a thought—and we have hundreds, or even thousands, of thoughts a day! With focused attention, **many of your thoughts can be creative,** whether it be imagining the next thing to check off your to-do list, seeing yourself completing homework quickly and accurately so you can move on to writing a song, or envisioning a community service day that you would like to organize.

Did you know that there are many ways to make change through your creative ideas? Try to use one or more of these methods to communicate about an issue that matters to you.

VISUAL ARTS
* Create T-shirts, posters, bumper stickers, and more (like many of the projects in this book!)

WRITING
* Write an op-ed, poem, essay, short story, or PSA (like the project on page 62)

THEATER ARTS & FILM
* Make or perform in a play or short film—documentary or fiction

MUSIC
* Write a song or musical, or host a benefit concert

COOKING
* Hold a bake sale, baking contest, or benefit dinner, or cook a meal for a senior citizen or family in need

LEADERSHIP
* Organize a team of volunteers to work together on an issue you care about
* Run for student office or start a social action club
* Start a book, article, movie, or conversation club that meets to learn about and discuss social issues

FASHION
* Find someone who is starting at a new job, recovering from cancer, or a new mom and help her find her personal style and revamp her wardrobe

INSPIRED STORY

When he was a college student at UC Santa Cruz, Brett Dennen worked with Lara Mendel, the Co-Founder of The Mosaic Project, to write many of the songs on the album *Children's Songs for Peace and a Better World*. The songs teach children worldwide how to empathize and resolve conflicts peacefully.

- Hold a back-to-school clothing drive to donate stylish clothes to kids who can't afford them
- Hold a fashion show fundraiser to raise money for clothing for people in need in your community

BUSINESS
- Start a business related to an issue that you care about

SPIRITUALITY
- Organize an interfaith picnic or youth group
- Write an article, speech, or song to share with your faith community

INSPIRED STORY

Shana Friedenberg, age 14, started Scarfadoodles, a puppy biscuit company that benefits shelter animals in her community.

BUT I'M NOT CREATIVE!

Everyone is creative. Just by living, you are creating your own life every day. Visual and graphic arts are just tools that allow you to express your innate creativity.

You don't have to wait until inspiration strikes to be creative. You can create the right conditions for creativity to flow. Here are just a few ways that work for us.

- Go on an inspiration rampage: Look on Pinterest and other sites for ideas that inspire you, and read books or articles about issues that you care about
- Brainstorm with a friend
- Make an inspiration board
- Do something that allows your mind to wander, like listening to music or going for a walk
- Keep a journal by your bedside—sometimes our best ideas come as we're falling asleep!

"Without leaps of imagination, or dreaming, we lose the excitement of possibilities. Dreaming, after all, is a form of planning."
—Gloria Steinem

SECTION THREE:

From INSPIRATION to INSPIRED ACTION

"We all do better
when we all do better."
-Paul Wellstone

HOW CAN I TAKE ACTION?

People come up with great ideas all the time. It's when they break a big idea into small, doable steps that you see real results. **That's why every creative vision needs a plan of action!**

Your inspired actions do not take place in a vacuum. They happen in the context of history and the world around you. To ensure your actions are relevant and successful, take the time to understand what has gone before and the forces that are at work now.

THE BODY POLITIC

No matter where you live, there are three main areas where you can have influence:

CULTURE

Culture is our collective beliefs, traditions, experiences, assumptions, likes, and dislikes. Every country has a culture. So do different groups, schools, and even families!

Often, culture is the first thing to change. Once culture changes, other things follow—such as laws and the way businesses operate.

Questions to consider:

* What are your culture's dominant values or beliefs about issues you care about, and how do they make you feel?
* How do these values or beliefs affect how people treat one another? How do they affect what people watch, buy, wear, listen to, or read?
* What would you like to change?
* What would you like to learn more about?

Ways to make change in culture:

* Post about an issue you care about on social media
* Design or wear a cause-related T-shirt or button
* Write a song, article, story, or speech
* Make a video
* Organize a club or action group
* Run for office at your school
* Have a conversation about an issue you care about with someone who has a different culture or viewpoint

ECONOMY

The economy is the means by which resources are distributed locally, nationally, and globally. Players in the economy include governments that create money supply and set the rules for trading, businesses that make and sell goods and provide jobs, and nonprofits that carry out social missions. Workers play a role, and so do you, by what you choose to buy, eat, and wear!

Questions to consider:

* What companies do you purchase goods from?
* How do these goods make you feel and why?
* How do the companies that make these goods treat customers, workers, suppliers, the environment, and their communities?
* What are some companies that are acting in a way that makes you feel good?
* How can you encourage more people to support these companies?
* Are there any needs that are not being met by companies or nonprofits in your community, and what could you do to help meet these needs?

Ways to make change in the economy:

* Buy from companies whose actions—not just their products—make you feel good
* Boycott businesses whose actions don't make you feel good
* Post on social media about companies you support
* Donate to nonprofits whose work you believe in
* Start a business or nonprofit yourself!

GOVERNMENT

Governments make the rules for cities, states, and countries. They also create institutions, such as courts and parliaments or congresses, that help people live together peacefully.

Governments provide public goods, like roads, parks, public transportation, national defense, clean water, waste removal, and law enforcement. They also protect basic rights, like clean air, clean water, and human rights.

Governments tend to move more slowly than businesses or culture, but they can change lives at a large scale since their laws and institutions govern and serve everyone.

Questions to consider:

* How does your government work? What are its rules and structures? How are laws passed?
* How are officials elected or put in charge?
* When do elections happen? How do they happen?
* How does your government listen to and respond to the needs of its citizens?
* What are some ways that citizens can make their voices heard?
* What does your government spend taxpayer money on?
  What are the largest expenses? What are the smallest?
* What surprises you about how money is spent?
  How would you spend it differently?
* How do people measure how well government is doing?
  What does the data show?
* Which leaders in your government do you admire or support? Why?
* How can you imagine your government working better?

Ways to make change in the government:

* Vote (if you're old enough) and encourage others to vote
* Let your representative know how you feel about issues you care about
* Attend a community or town hall meeting and speak out
* Volunteer for a campaign or political party
* Make and/or put up yard signs or bumper stickers
* Raise or give money to a campaign
* Answer a poll
* Write an opinion article
* Attend or organize a march or rally
* Run for office

VOTE WITH YOUR...VOTE!

Did you know that roughly 22 million teens will be eligible to vote in their first U.S. presidential election in 2020? And did you know that America has one of the lowest voter turnout rates of any developed country? (It's even lower in state and local elections!) (Source: Pew Research) Young people also show up at the lowest rates of all. You can make a real difference by getting out the vote! Here's how:

* Register people to vote. Once they're registered, about 85% to 88% of them vote! (Source: Pew Research)
* Volunteer with groups like Headcount, which works with musicians to put on concerts that promote youth voting and civic participation
* Go door-to-door at election time
* Talk to family and voting-age friends about the importance of voting
* See page 74 for a get-out-the-vote project!

VOTE WITH YOUR WALLET!

Socially conscious businesses, such as Patagonia, Clif Bar, Warby Parker, Yoobi, Cheeky Home, and Thinx, are becoming increasingly popular. They give you the power to vote with your wallet. If you can, support businesses that give back and take care of their workers, the environment, and your community. Check out their websites, talk to owners and employees, and read up about them online to learn more!

POLITICS, SCHMOLITICS!

We all want similar things in life. In general, we want to be happy and healthy, and we want as few people to suffer as possible. More specifically, we might want clean air and water, crime-free streets, or even healthier options in the cafeteria. The argument is how to achieve these things...enter politics!

Decisions that affect people within a group or community get made through politics. Politics is part of any culture, and can be seen in small groups and large communities alike. Elected officials use politics to achieve goals that address the needs and wants of all community members. That's why it's important to make your voice heard (see page 70)! Smaller scale examples include clubs, organizations, and student council (see page 48). Larger scale examples include city, state, and federal governments.

As you've probably noticed by reading the headlines, politics can bring out the best in people—strength, courage, service—but it sometimes brings out the worst too! Politics can rile people up because government decisions affect *everyone*. If the government is going to tell us what to do, we naturally want to have a say in it.

We believe that politics brings out the worst when individuals put their political party and identity labels first, such as race, class, income, gender, sexual orientation, or ethnicity, over *consciousness*, which is an acute awareness of your inner power in the present moment. **A conscious person understands that we are all interconnected,** each with valid views and worth, and plenty of common ground.

THREE POLITICAL AXES

Political parties are organized around different ways of thinking about how to achieve the things we want. Jonathan Haidt, Arnold Kling, and other political scholars have come up with simple frameworks to help us understand the three main political philosophies: Progressive, Libertarian, and Conservative.

Most people choose their political philosophy based on what they care about most. Arnold Kling says that people tend to act according to a **dominant axis**—a trade-off between two ideas. On one end of the axis is what you want. On the other end is what you *don't* want. When people make decisions, they tend to rely on their dominant axis to make a quick decision.

For Progressives, the dominant axis is **Care vs. Harm.** Progressives tend to prioritize caring about people, animals, and the planet—and not harming them. They tend to be concerned about care for the sick and vulnerable, including children, the elderly, the poor, and immigrants and refugees. They also tend to believe that it's the government's job to take care of its citizens.

For Libertarians (known as liberals outside of the U.S.), the dominant axis is **Freedom vs. Coercion.** Libertarians tend to prioritize protecting people's freedom. They want to avoid a government that controls your life. They tend to believe that it is not the government's role to care for people; that's what family and friends and charitable organizations are there for. They tend to favor minimal government intervention in private life and enterprise.

For Conservatives, the dominant axis is **Civilization vs. Barbarism.** Conservatives prioritize preserving the institutions and traditions that reflect a civilized society—for example, a society that is highly advanced in culture, science, industry, and government. Conservatives tend to value tradition (if it ain't broke, don't fix it because new solutions can introduce new problems) and can be cautious about change.

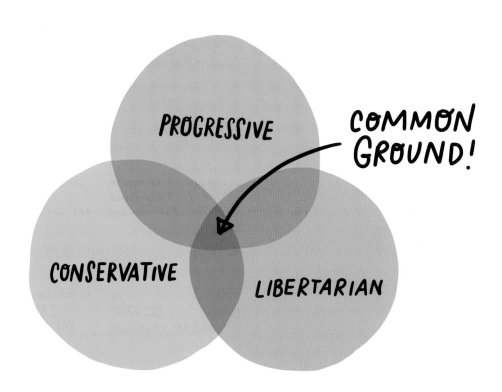

PROGRESSIVE

COMMON GROUND!

CONSERVATIVE

LIBERTARIAN

Conservatives, Libertarians, and Progressives each offer a valid, valuable perspective. When we disagree, it's important to look for connections and common ground. The reality is that most people hold a mix of conservative, libertarian, and progressive values, and **we need a harmonious balance** of *all* of these points of view to create a healthy society.

Despite the challenges of politics, it's an exciting time to get involved. As more people become better at resolving conflicts peacefully (see page 34), they are using their social media and online connections to relate to others. At the same time, technology, supported by people cooperating to solve problems, is demonstrating its potential to help solve many of the world's biggest problems, from hunger and poverty to global warming and cancer. **You can help lead the way!**

10 STEPS TO ORGANIZING
FOR CIVIC AND COMMUNITY ACTION

1 Pick your issue

Decide what issue you want to focus on. Questions to consider:

* What do I care about most?
* What issues have affected me personally?
* How do I like to spend my free time?
* What are my top concerns for my community/country?

2 Do your research and brainstorm solutions

To be the change, you have to see the change. Questions to consider:

* What is the situation/opportunity?
* If you're looking to help a group of people, what do they say they want or need?
* What have other people tried? What's been successful?
* What is realistic for me to do (time, money, talent)?
* Who do I know who could help?

When researching issues, it can be easy to pop on poop-colored goggles that trap you in a downward spiral of dystopian despair. Take them off. We live in a world of abundance. Trust that there is plenty for everyone. Focus on solutions, not on problems.

Next, imagine what you do want (e.g., every child with a full belly), not what you don't want (e.g., no child hungry). It's a subtle difference, but the first example brings to mind happy, healthy kids while the latter makes you think of hungry children—exactly what you don't want! Our thoughts become our reality, so keep them positive.

Finally, get every single silly hair-brained scheme down on paper. Pay attention to how the idea feels—if it feels realistic, it has a better chance of happening.

Need more service project ideas? Check out *The Kid's Guide to Service Projects: Over 500 Service Ideas for Young People Who Want to Make a Difference* by Barbara A. Lewis (Free Spirit, 2009).

What I Notice Now	Vision for the Future	Possible Actions
Americans waste 33 million tons of food a year—about ⅓ of the food we produce—while each year 36 million people around the world die of hunger. (Sources: USDA and The World Counts)	Everyone eats only what they need. Everyone has enough to eat!	**Brainstorm ideas** • Monitor our family's food waste and see where we can cut back • Make fridge magnets and pass them out at my school or church • Organize a volunteer day at my local food bank • Organize a canned food drive at my school • Cook a meal for an elderly person

3 Recruit a Dream Team

Being the change is more fun with friends, so invite some to join your dream team!

* Choose people you enjoy hanging out with, and who will stick with the project
* Don't limit yourself to people your own age. Consider inviting younger kids, college students, or older people to join you
* Reach out to nonprofit organizations and groups with similar interests
* Stay open to bringing new friends and allies to your cause. It's a cause, not a club!

4 Make an action plan

Figure out time lines, budgets, and tasks. Questions to consider:

* What inputs will we need (e.g., materials, money, allies, time)?
* What will we do? When? Who for or with?
* How will we measure results? Over what time period?
* What are the next steps (e.g., find an advisor, raise money)?

5 Find a sponsor or advisor

Ask a responsible adult (e.g., parent, teacher, community leader, family friend, etc.) to be your sponsor. They can help you navigate government offices, accompany you to town hall meetings, and/or give you credibility with other adults whose permission or support you might need. They can also turn into donors (if your project needs cash)!

6 Get Permission

Get any permissions you need to proceed with your activities.
For example:

* Your parents
* Your teacher or principal
* School district or city personnel
* Neighbors
* Owners of property you'd like to use
* Community organizations
* The people you want to serve if you are organizing a community service project
* Participants who appear in videos or photos to be shared online
* Anyone else?

7 Advertise

Let people know about your project and invite them to get involved.

* Make a PSA flyer to hand out (see page 62)
* Share your project on social media
* Host a community organizing meeting (see page 43)

8 Fun-draise

Does your project need cash? Here are some fun ways to raise $$$!

* Set up a lemonade stand, bake sale, or yard sale; donate 100% of the proceeds
* Host an ice cream social or pizza party with food donated by local businesses
* Set up an Indiegogo or GoFundMe campaign
* Ask for donations instead of gifts for your birthday or holidays
* Host a talent show or game show
* Host a walk-a-thon, fun run, or charity sporting event
* Do something daring or challenging for charity, like dying your hair a crazy color (with your parents' permission!), or giving up your phone for a month

9 Evaluate

Collect data during and after your project, then reflect on it with your team, advisors, family, and friends. Questions to consider:

* How did you feel after completing the project?
* How many people were affected? What was their response?
* Would you do it again?
* What would you do differently next time?

Ways to collect data include: observation (e.g., counting the number of people who attend an event), photographs, surveys, interviews and informal conversations, and social media metrics (e.g., likes and shares).

10 Repeat!

Experience is a great teacher, so use the lessons learned from your project to create even more impact with your next idea. Practice makes progress!

HOW TO HANDLE CONFLICT

Change often comes with conflict. However, conflict can be peaceful. The Mosaic Project, a youth empowerment organization, teaches these three keys to peaceful conflict resolution:

* **Listening.** Pay attention to the person's body language, what they say, and how they say it. Listen with your whole body.
* **Empathy.** Try to stand in the other person's shoes. Their shoes may not fit you perfectly, and that's okay. Do your best.
* **Assertive communication.** Being assertive means being strong without being mean. Learn to say "no"—a "no" to someone else is a "yes" to you!

To resolve a conflict peacefully, follow these five steps:

1. **Stop.** Cool off. Take a deep breath.

2. **Listen to each other.** Find out what you both need.

3. **Talk.** Use I-Statements (e.g., I feel... when I... so you could please...) instead of You-statements (e.g., You always...) which blame and give your power away.

4. **Empathize.** Really try to understand how the other person feels.

5. **Plan.** Brainstorm solutions and agree on a plan. Remember, it's not "you and me against each other," it's "you and me against the problem."

Living Room Conversations are a great tool for bridging divides. Four to six people with diverse viewpoints have a live or video conversation using the following guidelines:

* Be Curious and Open to Learning
* Show Respect and Suspend Judgment
* Look for Common Ground and Appreciate Differences
* Be Authentic and Welcome that from Others
* Be Purposeful and to the Point
* Own and Guide the Conversation

Write your own Living Room Conversation guide on pages 36-37.

BE THE CHANGE ON SOCIAL MEDIA

More people are using our interconnectedness online to foster empathy and cooperation, rather than allowing it to divide and polarize. Why not join them?

Social media is a powerful place to be the change. You can use it to:

- ✳ Connect with friends and family
- ✳ Connect with people who are different from you
- ✳ Share positive images—your highlight reel and selfies aren't selfish, they're a way to focus on what's positive in your life!
- ✳ Model kind behavior—be happy for others, comfort them when they're down
- ✳ Spread the word about causes you believe in and share inspiration

Social media also presents challenges. Here's how you can turn them into positives:

- ✳ Don't respond to negative comments, or if you do, simply say "thank you" or "thank you, and here's how I see it..."
- ✳ Don't re-post items that make you feel shocked or angry, or that confirm a strong belief or fear. Double check the item's claims and think about its intent
- ✳ Turn FOMO (fear of missing out) into NOMO (necessity of missing out). You can't physically do everything and be everywhere, so you'll have to make choices and miss out sometimes! When your friends are having fun without you, question your anxious or jealous thoughts. Joy comes from within.

Living Room Conversation Guide

Use this guide to bring 4–7 people with different views together for a video or in-person conversation focused on listening. The more differently participants think, the more everyone learns! If you like, ask a parent or teacher to help you (teachers can sign up their class at Mismatch.org).

WELcome

Review the Conversation Ground Rules (page 34) together. Then introduce the issue you want to discuss (free speech on campus, girls' rights, income inequality, etc.). What seems to be the main source of disagreement? (some people believe...others believe...). Be neutral and try to imagine all sides of the issue.

_____

_____

_____

_____

ROUND 1:

GETTING STARTED

* What sense of purpose or duty guides you in your life?
* What do your friends say makes you tick?
* What are your hopes and concerns for your community/your country?

ROUND 2:

YOUR THOUGHTS, IDEAS, AND CONCERNS

Ask participants 3–5 open-ended questions about your topic.

* How did you first become interested in this topic?
* What personal experience comes to mind when you hear the topic debated?
* What is one issue related to the topic that you wish we could solve together?

ROUND 3:

REFLECTION

* In one sentence, what was most meaningful or valuable about this conversation?

Closing

Thank your participants and follow up on any action items.

CHANGE MAKERS

MARDY MURIE

Mardy Murie was born in 1902 and was the first woman to graduate from the University of Alaska. She and her husband Olaus dedicated their lives to environmental conservation, and their small acts and testimony before Congress helped to create the Arctic National Wildlife Refuge. There were days when they made no progress at all, but that didn't deter them. It was only when she was 96 years old that Mardy was recognized by President Bill Clinton with the Presidential Medal of Freedom, the United States' highest civilian honor!

NELSON MANDELA

Nelson Mandela was a South African revolutionary and political leader. He served as President of South Africa from 1994 to 1999, the country's first black head of state. Inspired by the stories of his ancestors during the wars of resistance, he vowed to fight for the freedom of his people. His government focused on tackling apartheid, a system of segregation based on race. He never wavered in his devotion to democracy and equality. He was regarded as a controversial figure for much of his life, having spent 27 years in prison. Through his life's work, he eventually gained international acclaim and received more than 250 honors, including the Nobel Peace Prize.

MARTIN LUTHER KING JR.

Martin Luther King Jr. was a passionate, positive champion for civil rights. While he did a huge amount to end segregation in the United States, he was assassinated just days before the passage of the landmark Civil Rights Act of 1968. Even today, the struggle for civil rights continues with a disproportionate number of African Americans in prison or living in poverty. His work continues to inspire millions worldwide.

DOLORES HUERTA

Dolores Huerta is a lifelong community organizer and champion of economic justice. In 1962, she co-founded the National Farm Workers Association to help farmworkers have better lives and wages. Dolores started out as a dedicated member of her local Girl Scouts chapter; her dedication and willingness to serve soon gave her huge responsibilities and opportunities to lead. While she at first planned to be a teacher, she realized she could change more lives by organizing them to stand up for changes they wanted to see. To this day, she is an activist for improving the lives of the working poor, women, and children.

THE DALAI LAMA

The 14th Dalai Lama was born Lhamo Thondup in 1935 in Takster, China to a peasant family. He became the spiritual and political leader of Tibet at age 15, just before the invasion by the People's Republic of China. As the exiled political leader of Tibet, he has worked towards the peaceful liberation of Tibet, and regularly speaks and writes about a wide range of topics, including peace, compassion, women's rights, preserving the environment, interfaith understanding, and the science of happiness and maintaining a healthy mind.

OLYMPIA SNOWE

U.S. Senator Olympia Snowe is a passionate advocate for listening and finding common ground. The youngest Republican woman ever to be elected to the U.S. House of Representatives, she was named one of America's best senators by *Time* magazine. In 2012, she decided to leave the Senate because it had grown too partisan. She founded Olympia's List, a group dedicated to supporting political candidates who are consensus-builders and want to be the change.

CRAIG KIELBURGER

Craig Kielburger was twelve years old when he opened the newspaper to a story about the murder of Iqbal Masih, a former child slave and child labor activist. After more research about child labor, Craig and his classmates collected 3,000 signatures for a petition to the prime minister of India that requested the release of imprisoned child-labor activist Kailash Satyarthi (who went on to win a Nobel Peace Prize). The petition was sent in a shoebox wrapped in brown paper. On his eventual release, Satyarthi said, "It was one of the most powerful actions taken on my behalf, and for me, definitely the most memorable." Craig and his brother Marc went on to found Free the Children, which today is Me to We, one of the largest youth activism and international development organizations in the world.

FLORENCE NIGHTINGALE

Florence Nightingale was an English social reformer and pioneer of professional nursing, paving the way for modern-day healthcare. Her revolutionary role started during the Crimean War, where she organized and tended to wounded soldiers. Following the war, she laid the groundwork for nursing by establishing the first ever scientifically based nursing school in London. Her social reforms greatly impacted the British healthcare system and destigmatized women in the workforce. She was the first woman awarded the Order of Merit. To recognize the important role of nurses in healthcare, her birthday is observed annually on International Nurses Day on May 12.

MALALA YOUSAFZAI

Malala Yousafzai was born in Pakistan in 1997. Soon after the Taliban took over in 2004, she noticed changes she did not like, like bans on TV, music, and women's rights to go shopping. The Taliban started to bomb girls' schools. Malala was so furious that she gave a speech in 2008 at age 11 titled, "How dare the Taliban take away my basic right to education?" In 2009, she began writing an anonymous blog for the BBC about living under Taliban rule. After her identity was revealed, she was shot in the head by a Taliban gunman. She survived the assassination attempt, and in 2014, she became the youngest person to receive the Nobel Peace Prize for her fight for youth empowerment and the right of all children to education. She is one of the world's leading education advocates.

PRINCESS Diana

Princess Diana is remembered as the "People's Princess." She defied the norms of British Royalty by using her fame to raise awareness for humanitarian causes worldwide. During her life, she changed the perception of the British monarchy and was quoted saying, "I would like a monarchy that has more contact with its people." It became her personal mission to connect with and change the lives of those in need. Her charitable efforts went beyond fundraising. She was known for her hospital visits and her great care for the young and vulnerable. She was an activist, an advocate, and an outstanding listener.

MOTHER TERESA

Mother Teresa, born Anjezë Gonxhe in Albania, was known for her love of the most vulnerable members of society. As a girl, she was fascinated by stories of missionaries and decided to become a nun. After moving to Calcutta, India, and witnessing the extreme poverty, she decided to devote her life to helping the poor. In 1950, she created the Missionaries of Charity, a group of women who opened hospices, orphanages, centers for the blind and disabled, and a leper colony. In 1979, Mother Teresa received the Nobel Peace Prize for her humanitarian work. Today, the Missionaries of Charity consists of over 4,500 sisters and continues to help the world's most vulnerable.

TAKE THE LONG VIEW

Being the change and making change is a marathon, not a sprint. Many of history's greatest change makers didn't see the results of their work in their own lifetime. And many of them didn't expect to. **Letting go of the idea that it's all up to you** gives you the freedom to take risks, set realistic goals, and keep a happy balance in your life between friends, family, health, faith, hobbies, school, and work.

We are all drops in the ocean—seemingly insignificant, yet capable of ripple effects beyond what we can imagine. **We are all part of bigger waves of change,** so go with the flow and see what happens!

"Every moment is an organizing opportunity, every person a potential activist, every minute a chance to change the world."
-Dolores Huerta

Additional Ways to Be the Change

HOST A COMMUNITY ORGANIZING MEETING

Community organizing meetings turn inspiration into action!

✳ Start planning your meeting about a month ahead and set clear goals

✳ Invite four times the amount of people you want to show up

✳ Get the word out on Facebook or Eventbrite, and text people a day or two before to remind them

✳ During your meeting, set a clear agenda and stick to it; keep it to about 1-1.5 hours

✳ Keep your message positive and communicate a clear time line, tactics, and path to victory

✳ Use paper sign-up forms to get contact info and on-the-spot volunteer commitments

✳ After your meeting, follow up with volunteers to make sure they complete their tasks; then start planning your next meeting!

WHAT TO BRING TO A PROTEST

Peaceful protests are an awesome way to show solidarity. Here's what to bring:

✳ An adult, if you're under 18!

✳ ID

✳ Paper with emergency contact and health info (e.g., allergies)

✳ Medication (if needed), and Band-Aids/first aid kit

✳ Cell phone

✳ Small amount of cash

✳ Water bottle

✳ Sunscreen

✳ Sunglasses

✳ Snacks

✳ Layers and comfy shoes

✳ A small bag or purse to carry it all (large backpacks may not be allowed)

✳ A sign! (see page 100)

HOW TO INFLUENCE YOUR REPRESENTATIVE

Elected officials want to hear from you. Their reelection relies on keeping voters happy! You can write a postcard (see page 70), make a phone call, drop into their local office, attend a town hall or community meeting, or message or post comments to them on social media. Remember, timing is everything. Reach out when they are actively working on a law or policy that you care about.

YOU FOR PRESIDENT!

Want to run for office someday? It's never too early to start preparing! To learn the ropes, volunteer for someone else's campaign, take on a leadership role at a school club, or run for student government. To run for office:

* Understand the office
    * What are the roles and responsibilities?
    * What qualifications are needed to do a good job?
* Know yourself
    * What are your strengths?
    * What are your weaknesses?
    * What are your core values?
    * How would you describe yourself in three words?
    * Why should someone vote for you?
* Garner support
    * Share your intent to run with friends and family and ask them for advice
    * Speak directly to as many of the people who would be voting for you as you can. Ask them what they care about
    * Listen, listen, listen
* Advertise and communicate
    * See page 48 for a campaign poster idea
    * Lead by example
* Show your enthusiasm!
    * Whether you win or lose, celebrate and congratulate the winner!
    * If you won, get ready to get to work!

SECTION FOUR:

CRAFT PROJECTS

"How wonderful it is that nobody need wait a single moment before starting to improve the world."
-Anne Frank

Tools and Materials

A great creative project starts with the right tools and materials. Here are some of our favorites.

CARDBOARD AND CARD STOCK

Cardboard is our favorite surface for making signs. It's cheap, easy to cut to any shape or size with a box cutter or craft knife, and won't warp if you paint it. Foam core and poster board also work well if you prefer a more polished look. For greeting card and postcard projects, we love keeping 80- to 100-lb card stock on hand in white and different colors, along with a stash of envelopes.

PAINT & SPRAY PAINT

Tempera paints in bright colors are a simple way to make a statement. We also love to use spray paint in bright neons on cardboard, poster board, and on fabric. MTN water-based spray paints are low odor, meaning you can do your project indoors. For detailed designs on fabric, like our Wild Feminist tote on page 82, we recommend textile paints— they're easy to use and won't come off in the wash.

PAINT PENS & PERMANENT MARKERS

We love paint pens and permanent markets for making posters and decorating surfaces, from vinyl to journal covers. They're bright, opaque, and fun to use for drawing and hand-lettering. For most of our projects, we used Sakura Permapaque®, Sharpie®, Uchida® Deco Color Paint, and Posca Paint Pens. Fine-tip permanent markers and felt-tip pens are great for detailed line work.

BRUSH-TIP PENS

Brush-tip pens give an artful, loose feel to anything you write.
Their tapered tips, which look just like the tip of a paintbrush,
allow you to change the width of your stroke as you write simply
by changing the angle and the amount of applied pressure.
Different stroke thicknesses on the down-strokes and cross-
strokes help achieve distinctive looks—which is the secret to
great hand-lettering! Our favorite brush-tip pen is the Tombow®
pen, which has a brush-tip on one end and a finer felt-tip on the
other. We also love Sakura Koi® Coloring Brush Pens for loose,
colorful illustrations.

GEL PENS

Gel pens are opaque, come in lots of great colors, and are fun
to draw with. We're partial to Sakura Gelly Roll® pens for their
vibrant neons and opaque whites, which make art on a dark
surface really pop.

T-SHIRTS, TOTES, AND MUGS

You can use any plain mugs, bags or T-shirts for your projects—
it's a great opportunity to upcycle! For our projects, we used
T-shirts from Alternative Apparel, which offers blank organic,
sustainable, ethically sourced T's in tons of great styles. Blank
ceramic mugs and totes are available online or at craft supply
stores. For the mug project in this book, we used enamelware
coffee mugs from Crow Canyon Home.

PIN-MAKING TOOLS

Clear epoxy stickers paired with a separate adhesive pin backing
(both available at craft stores and at online retailers) are an easy,
inexpensive way to make buttons. You can get epoxy stickers in
a variety of sizes. Consider getting a circle cutter to match your
favorite sticker size, or just use a circular object, like a coin or roll
of tape, to trace a circle shape.

ADHESIVE VINYL

Adhesive vinyl comes in lots of eye-catching colors (including
clear and glitter!), and is great for making any kind of handmade
sticker, including bumper stickers (page 52) and decals like the
Stay Bright switch plate (page 96).

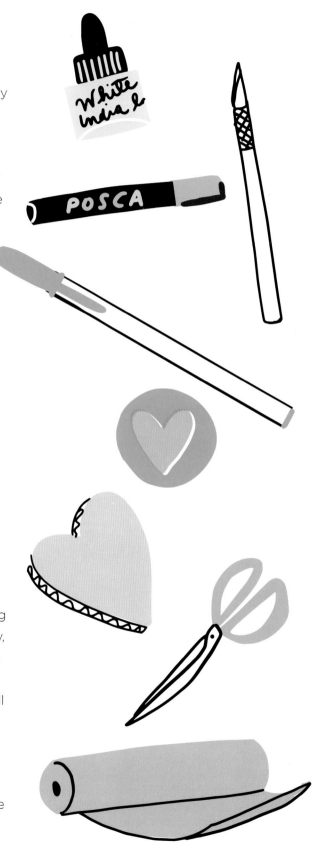

CAMPAIGN POSTER

Running for student government is an awesome way to experience public service and build your confidence as a leader. Getting elected is the first step, and that's where an eye-catching campaign poster comes in! These flyers are super easy to make—start with a selfie, photocopy it to get a cool zine-like graphic, add a hand-lettered campaign slogan, make copies to post around your school, and add eye-catching pops of color with a highlighter. Be yourself, have fun, and go get 'em!

WHAT YOU'LL NEED

* Sheet of 8½" x 11" printer paper
* Photo of yourself
* Pencil
* Eraser
* Scissors
* Variety of highlighters
* White gel pen
* White paint pen
* Black Tombow® ABT Brush Pen
* Computer and printer (optional)

CAMPAIGN SLOGAN IDEAS*

A Vote for Me is a Vote for You!

Vote _____ to Represent You!

When Put to the Test, I Will Be Best!

You Want Something Done, I am the One

Many People Agree, Vote for Me for VP!

Don't Worry, Be Happy, Vote _____ for President!

*Source: Shoutslogans.com

"One of the lessons that I grew up with was to always stay true to yourself and never let what somebody else says distract you from your goals. And so when I hear about negative and false attacks, I really don't invest any energy in them, because I know who I am." -Michelle Obama

INSTRUCTIONS

1. Size a photo of yourself (preferably taken against a white wall) to fit on a sheet of 8½" x 11" printer paper, leaving room at the top of the page for your message, and print out the photo.

2. With a pencil, write in your message to fit around your image. Using a black Tombow® pen (or other thick black marker), ink the message.

3. Make as many copies as you need, and decorate the copies by adding fun details with highlighters, white paint, and gel pencils.

TIP
Have a poster-making party to get your friends in on the action!

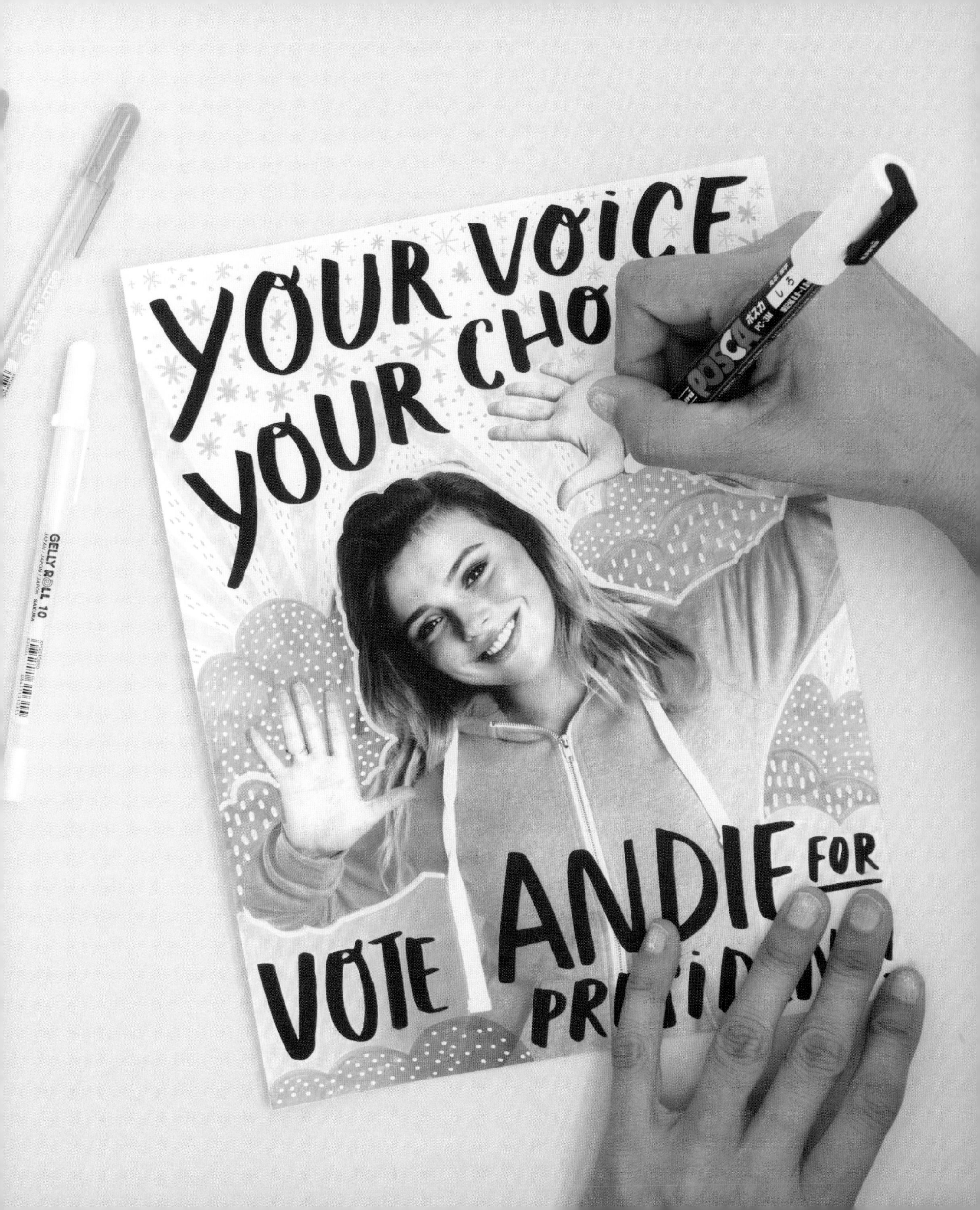
YOUR VOICE
VOTE
ANDIE FOR
GELLY ROLL 10
SAKURA
POSCA
PC-3M

WORD on THE STREET

BUMPER STICKERS

Did you know that Americans spend 300 hours a year driving in their cars? (Source: AAA Foundation) That's a lot of time that they could be thinking about how to be the change! Use adhesive-backed vinyl, available in many colors and finishes (including glitter), and paint markers to create positive bumper stickers. Turn road rage into road radiance!

WHAT YOU'LL NEED

* Adhesive-backed vinyl

* Pencil

* Scissors

* Uchida® Deco Color paint marker (Posca® pens, Sharpie® and other waterproof or oil-based pens work as well)

* Nail polish remover (optional)

* Cotton swabs (optional)

INSTRUCTIONS

1. Fold a piece of vinyl in half, and draw half a heart with a pencil. Cut out heart shape with scissors.

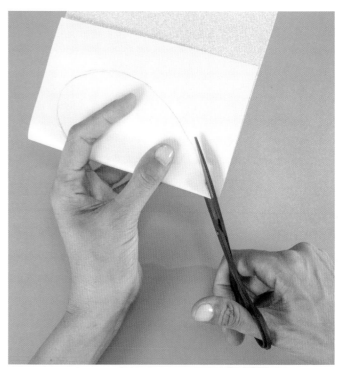

2. Add your message with a paint marker. If you are not comfortable free-handing, you can first sketch with a pencil, and then go over it with a paint marker. If needed, erase any mistakes with nail polish remover and a cotton swab.

3. Now your sticker is ready to be placed! Peel away 1 or 2 inches of the backing and stick it to your surface. Continue to smooth and peel until the entire sticker is in place.

SOME MESSAGE IDEAS

Save the Mermaids - Protect Our Oceans
(Mermaid and fish)

Peace is Possible
(Dove and heart)

Go Vote!
(Hands in the air)

Grl Pwr
(Rainbows or flowers)

Rescue is my Favorite Breed
(Dog or cat)

Let Equality Bloom
(Flowers)

Support Your Local Farmer
(Farm animal)

THERE IS NO PLANET B

WORDS TO LIVE BY

INSPIRATIONAL JOURNAL

Keeping a journal is a great way to stay centered. Map out projects, jot down ideas, set your intention for the day, week, or year, and keep track of your goals and progress. Personalize your own journal with a selfie and an inspirational quote to stay in tune with your vision.

WHAT YOU'LL NEED

* Photo of yourself

* White notebook

* A variety of pens that work on your notebook surface (We used Posca® paint pens, Sharpie® white water-based paint pen, and a black fine point Sharpie®)

* Scissors

* Glue stick

> "Every individual matters. Every individual has a role to play. Every individual makes a difference."
> –Jane Goodall

IDEAS TO WRITE DOWN IN YOUR JOURNAL
• Your top three goals for the day, week, or year
• Your schedule for the day, from wake-up to bedtime
• What you're grateful for today
• Issues you feel passionate about or are curious to learn more about
• Your creative talents, and how you can use them to be the change
• Your (s)heroes
• Your representatives and community leaders
• Quotes that inspire you
• Books, documentaries, podcasts, and articles you'd like to check out

1. Cut out your selfie so it lines up with the corner of the notebook, and then glue the photo to the front of the book.

2. With a pencil, lightly write out your inspirational quote.

3. When you are happy with your sketch, ink the quote with a black Sharpie®, and then decorate the rest of the notebook with a variety of pens.

TIP

To have your selfie fit the cover perfectly, line the photo up to the corner of the notebook. Flip the notebook over and trace the corner onto the back of your photo with a pencil, and then cut the photo to size.

TEAMWORK MAKES THE DREAM WORK

TEAM T-SHIRT

Walks, runs, bike-rides, and other fitness activities are a great way to have fun while raising money and awareness for a cause. Get your friends together and give yourselves a team name. Then, motivate and reward your team by making your own team T-shirt! When it comes to being the change, teamwork really does make the dream work!

WHAT YOU'LL NEED

For stencils

* Large sheet of adhesive vinyl (we used a 12" x 15" sheet)
* 12" x 15" or larger sheet of cardboard
* 8½" x 11" sheet of card stock or photo paper
* Scissors
* Pencil
* Craft knife
* Cutting mat
* Computer and printer (optional)
* Font (optional-PaperCute available on myfonts.com)

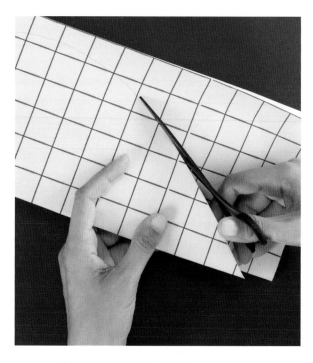

For stenciling T-shirt(s)

* White T-shirt(s)
* Scrap cardboard
* Extra scrap paper
* Spray adhesive
* Iron
* Ironing board
* Spray paint in neon red, pink, and yellow (we like MTN water-based spray paints because they are low odor)
* Masking tape (optional)

INSTRUCTIONS

1. Prewash all T-shirts.

2. Fold your large sheet of adhesive vinyl in half and draw half a heart, sized to fit on your T-shirt. Cut it out with scissors and unfold. This will be your stencil.

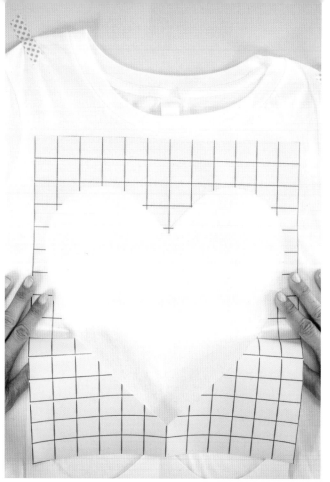

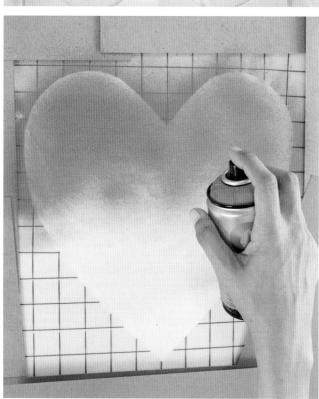

③ Cut a piece of cardboard larger than your stencil to fit inside the shirt and insert it. This will prevent the spray paint from bleeding to the other side.

④ Cover any exposed areas around the stencil with scrap paper. Secure with masking tape (optional). Spray from directly above with the spray paint. Add several coats to get even and solid coverage, allowing each coat to dry a bit before adding another. Carefully remove the stencil and scrap paper. Allow to dry to the touch before working on the back.

⑤ For the back stencil, hand letter the message on an 8½" x 11" sheet of card stock paper, or type it on a computer using a simple font. (We used PaperCute Bold, the perfect font for stenciling because you don't have to worry about the inner cut outs.)

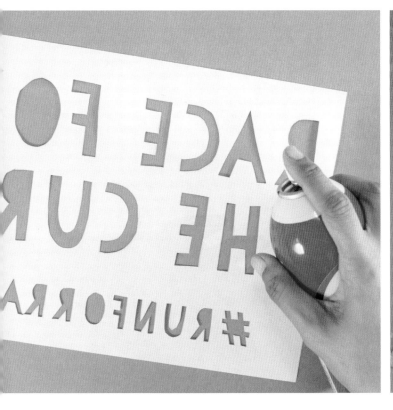

6. With a craft knife on a cutting mat or magazine, carefully cut out the letters.

7. Cover the back of the stencil with spray adhesive, and position the stencil on the back of the T-shirt (with the cardboard still inside). Spray adhesive will help you get a crisp print.

8. Cover any exposed areas around the stencil with scrap paper, tucking the paper under the edges of the stencil to help hold them in place.

9. Spray the stencil with stripes of red, pink, and yellow spray paint to create a subtle rainbow effect.

10. To set the color, iron both sides of the shirt with a hot iron for at least 30 seconds at the temperature best suited to the fabric (we used a tea towel between the T-shirt and iron to keep from mucking up the iron).

TIPS

Always wash your shirts inside out to prevent fading.

*

If you're making several shirts, paint all the fronts first and then all the backs for efficiency.

KNOWLEDGE is POWER

PSA POSTER

PSAs, or public service announcements, are short messages in the form of a poster, video, or audio recording. They're a catchy, quick way to bring people up to speed on an issue and invite them to take action. You can hang PSA posters on bulletin boards or telephone poles, turn them into graphics to post on social media, hand them out at farmer's markets, or even place them on neighbor's doorsteps. You can send a video or audio PSA to your local TV or radio station, or your favorite podcast. Be sure to include a written script in case the host wants to read it on air!

WHAT YOU'LL NEED

* 8½" x 11" printer paper

* Neon copy paper

* Pencil

* Eraser

* A variety of black markers in different sizes (We used Sharpie®, Tombow® ABT Brush Pen, Permapaque® markers, among others)

SAMPLE PSA TOPICS

• Voting
• Discrimination
• Gun safety
• Healthy eating
• Drinking and driving
• Texting and driving
• Suicide prevention
• Animal cruelty
• Girls' rights

TIPS

Think of a hook, i.e., an idea or tagline, that will grab people's attention

Research a few key facts to frame the situation

Offer a clear solution and call to action

Use bold colors

Keep it short—less is more!

Involve experts or people in your target audience in your brainstorming

INSTRUCTIONS

1. Pencil in your message using a variety of sizes and styles of lettering in order to fill up the page. Add appropriate doodles, frames, lines, and other flair to fill in any open space.

2. Have your flyer copied on neon copy paper and distribute. You can also snap a photo pf your PSA and share on social media.

MANY THANKS!

DOODLED THANK YOU NOTE

Keep an attitude of gratitude! When you're organizing volunteers or asking for support for a cause, it is hugely important to say thank you. A handwritten note is the best way to show your appreciation. Doodle a thank you note and choose a message that relates to your cause, then reproduce it so you always have a stash on hand!

WHAT YOU'LL NEED

* 8½" x 11" sheet of dark blue or black card stock

* White Gelly Roll® pen

* White India Ink (we used Dr. Ph Martin's Bombay White India Ink)

* #2 round paint brush

* Craft knife

* Cutting mat or magazine

* Ruler

* Pencil

* A7 envelope

Other IDEAS

* You're awesome sauce! Thanks! (Jars of sauce)

* Together, we CAN make a difference! Thanks! (Cans of food)

* Warmest thanks! (Hats, mittens and gloves)

* Thanks for your time! (Clocks)

* It's OWL thanks to you! (Owls)

* Thanks for lending a hand! (Hands)

* Thanks for the love! (Hearts)

* You're paw-some! Thanks! (Dogs or cats)

* Mega thanks! (Megaphones)

INSTRUCTIONS

1. Make your card! Fold card stock in half horizontally. With a ruler and craft knife, cut the card down to 5" x 7" folded.

2. With a ruler and pencil, mark horizontal lines and lightly pencil in the message and pattern.

3. With a brush and the white ink, ink the pattern and text. Go over areas twice where needed.

4. Once it is dry, write a note on the inside with a white Gelly Roll® pen. Pop it in an envelope and mail or hand-deliver!

WHAT TO WRITE IN A THANK YOU NOTE

Keep it simple, specific, and sincere!
Here's an example:

> Dear Kara,
>
> Thank you so much for volunteering with me at the food bank last week. I can't believe we sorted 50,000 pounds of oranges! I loved getting the chance to help our community AND hang out with you. You are such an awesome friend! Thank you!
>
> XOXO
>
> Jane

EASY AS PIE!

DONATION JAR

A great pun puts the "fun" in fundraising! Use your hand-lettering and doodling skills to create a donation jar to raise cash for your favorite cause! This project was inspired by Mason Wartman, the 27 year-old owner of Rosa's Fresh Pizza in Philadelphia. Customers at Rosa's can donate $1 to serve a slice of pizza to a homeless person. Rosa's feeds 50-100 homeless people a day!

WHAT YOU'LL NEED

* Large jar
* White card stock
* Neon pink Gelly Roll® pen or highlighter
* Black charcoal pencil or crayon
* Pencil
* Scissors
* Ruler
* Small plate (we used a 6" plate)
* A quarter, washi tape roll, or other small circular object for tracing pepperoni shapes
* White glue
* Double-sided tape
* Small piece of cardboard or foam core (optional)

TIP

If you're placing your jar at a local business, make sure to get their permission first!

INSTRUCTIONS

1. With a ruler and pencil, draw a pizza-shaped triangle on a piece of card stock. Use a small round object, like a tape roll or coin, to trace circles for the pepperoni.

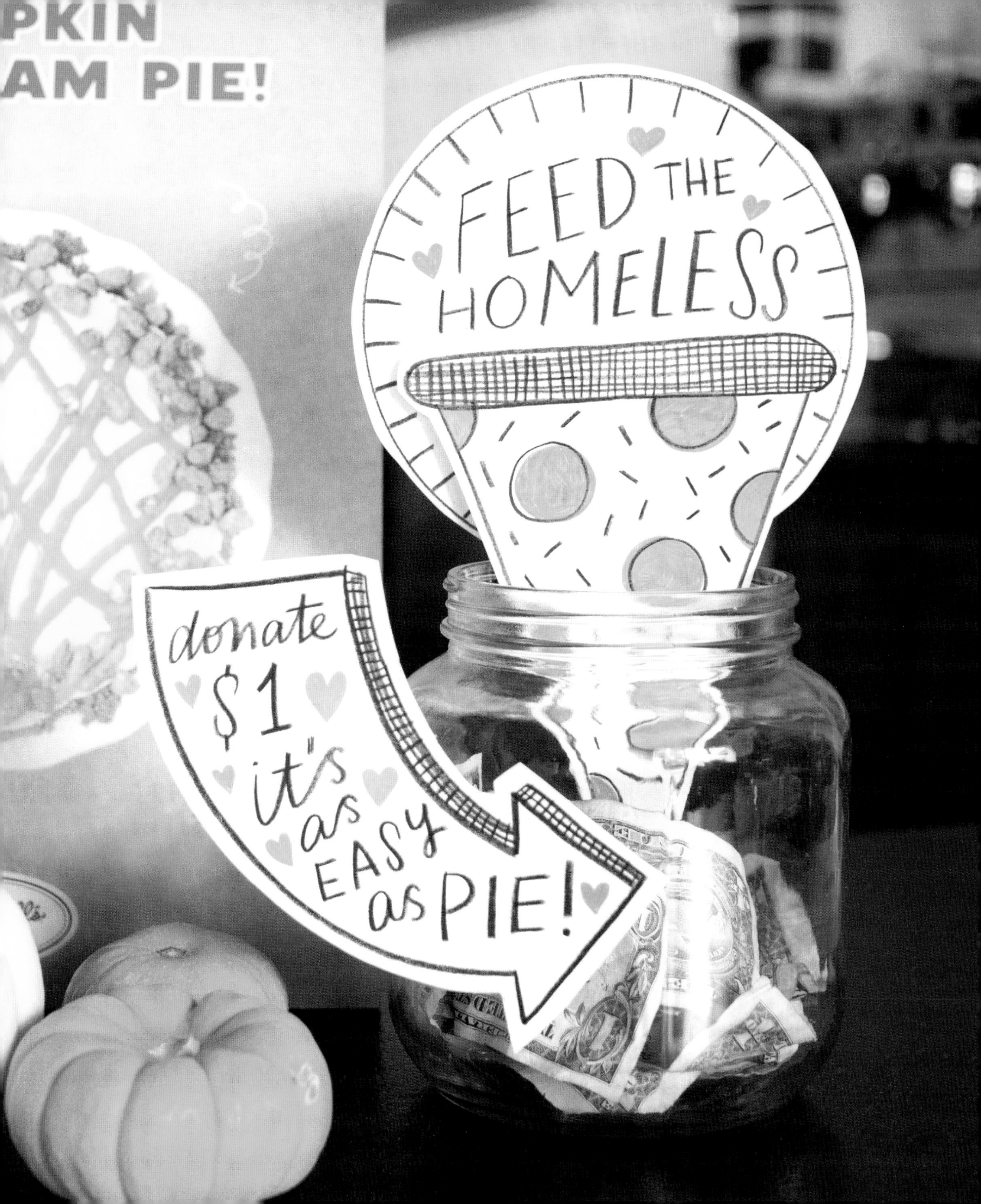
PKIN
AM PIE!
FEED THE HOMELESS
donate $1 it's as EASY as PIE!

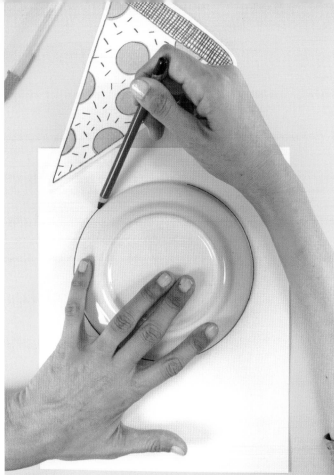

2 Color in the pepperoni with a neon pink Gelly Roll® pen (a pink highlighter will also work).

3 Using a black charcoal pencil or crayon, draw the outline of the pizza, pepperoni, and crust, and then add some short lines sprinkled throughout. Cut out the shape with a pair of scissors, leaving a bit of a white border.

4 Place a small plate on a piece of card stock and trace a circle with the black crayon.

5 Draw lines around the edge of the circle to make it look like a paper plate. Position the slice of pizza to overlap the plate, and then pencil in the text. Draw in text with black crayon and add some hearts with the Gelly Roll® pen. Cut out the plate leaving a slight border.

6 Optionally, glue a small piece of cardboard or foam core to the plate and glue the pizza to it to add a little dimension.

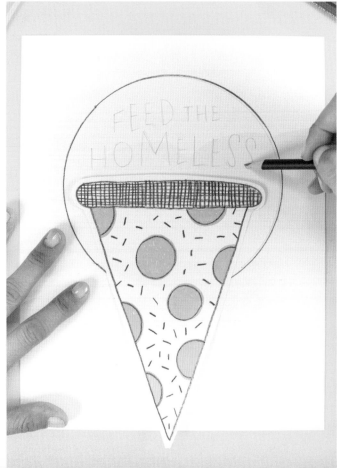

7. On a sheet of card stock, draw an arrow sized to fit your jar, and then pencil in the lettering. Trace your drawing with a black crayon. Add a few neon pink hearts. Cut out the shape with scissors.

8. Attach the pizza and arrow shape to your jar using double-sided tape.

Other IDEAS

Be Pawsome Today!
(Animal's paw)

Be a Hero!
(Medal or superhero fist)

Change the World! Every penny counts! (Penny)

VOTE YES/VOTE NO

POSTCARD TO YOUR REPRESENTATIVE

Legislators are busy people! They are more likely to listen and respond to a short, simple, and bold statement about a bill they are actively working on. "Vote No" or "Vote Yes" makes a clear statement, and a bright pattern makes your message really pop. Representatives keep a tally of the number of calls and letters they get, so why not throw a postcard making party? There's power and creativity in numbers!

WHAT YOU'LL NEED

* 8½" x 11" sheet of heavy white card stock (we used 110 lb)

* Neon fine point Sharpie® markers

* Sakura Permapaque® markers

* Posca medium tip paint pens

* Craft knife

* Cutting mat or magazine

* Ruler

* Pencil

* Postage stamp

INSTRUCTIONS

1. Make your postcard! Trim down white card stock to 5" x 7".

2. With a neon pink Sharpie®, draw abstract blobs across the card.

3. Add yellow blobs in between the pink to create an all-over pattern. We used a yellow Sakura Permapaque® marker.

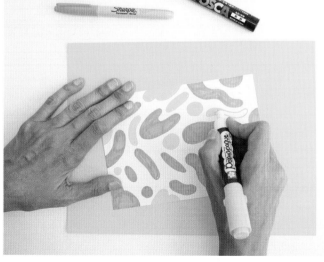

4 With a ruler and a pencil, mark straight lines (as many as you need to fit your message) to indicate where your type with go. Lightly pencil in the letters to make sure they fit and that you like the placement.

5 With a blue paint pen (we used a Posca® medium tip paint pen), write your message. Then draw the leaf pattern over the pink and yellow background pattern.

6 Decorate the back of the postcard and write a short message.

7 Address it to your representative, add postage, and pop your card in the mail!

WRITING TIPS

* Address your postcard using a respectful prefix, such as The Honorable, Mr./Ms./Mrs., or Senator or Representative.

* Write legibly.

* State your concern in one short sentence, e.g., "I support the passage of Bill XYZ," "Thank you for your support of Bill XYZ," or "Bill XYZ should not be allowed to pass."

* Back up your concern with a short statistic or personal experience.

* Close your note respectfully, with "Thank you," "Sincerely," or "Yours truly."

* Include your name and return address so they can verify that you are one of their constituents and contact you if needed!

TIP

You'll probably get a form response back. Don't be offended—
elected officials are busy! You made your voice heard, and that's what counts!

Other IDEAS

* Health care: bandages, stethoscopes, red crosses, hearts

* Aid for the poor or homeless: fresh fruits & veggies, hats & mittens, houses

* Aid for children: baby bottles, kites, toys, dolls

* Equal rights: hearts, rainbows, faces of different people

* Science, energy, and innovation: rocket ships, robots, atoms, planets and stars

* The environment: animals, parks, clouds, water

* Education: apples, pencils, rulers, award ribbons

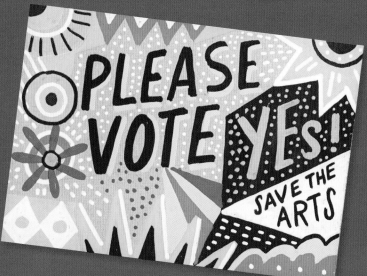

THE FUTURE is in YOUR HANDS

IRON-ON T-SHIRT

Young people are the future when it comes to voting! In 2016, Millennials (age 19-35) started to outnumber Baby Boomers (age 52-70) in the U.S. They'll soon be the largest voter group! The bad news? Young people are not showing up to vote! In 2016, only 49% of eligible Millennial voters turned out compared to 62–70% of older generations. (Source: Pew Research) Use this T-shirt, along with volunteering, to send more of your peers to the polls!

WHAT YOU'LL NEED

* Blank T-shirt

* Therm O Web® Heat'n Bond Ultra Hold Iron-On Adhesive

* ½" yard black cotton

* White Jacquard® textile paint

* Round brush (size 2 or smaller)

* Light colored fabric chalk

* Ballpoint pen

* Sharp scissors

* Iron

* Ironing board

INSTRUCTIONS

1 Cut a piece of black cotton big enough to fit all the design templates on pages 105–107. Following the instructions for the iron-on adhesive, apply the adhesive to the fabric with an iron.

2 Cut out the templates. Cover the back of each template with light-colored fabric chalk. Place each template on your black cotton, chalk-side down, and trace over the design with a ball point pen, pressing firmly. This will transfer the design onto your fabric.

3 With sharp scissors, cut out the separate design elements (hands, crystal ball, base, stars, lightning bolts, "VOTE" letters).

4 Sketch details and lettering on each element with fabric chalk. Then paint on the details and fill in the lettering with white fabric paint. Let dry completely.

5 Position the design elements on the T-shirt and iron on with a hot iron, following instructions for the adhesive. You can place the entire design on the shirt at the same time, or iron on one element at time.

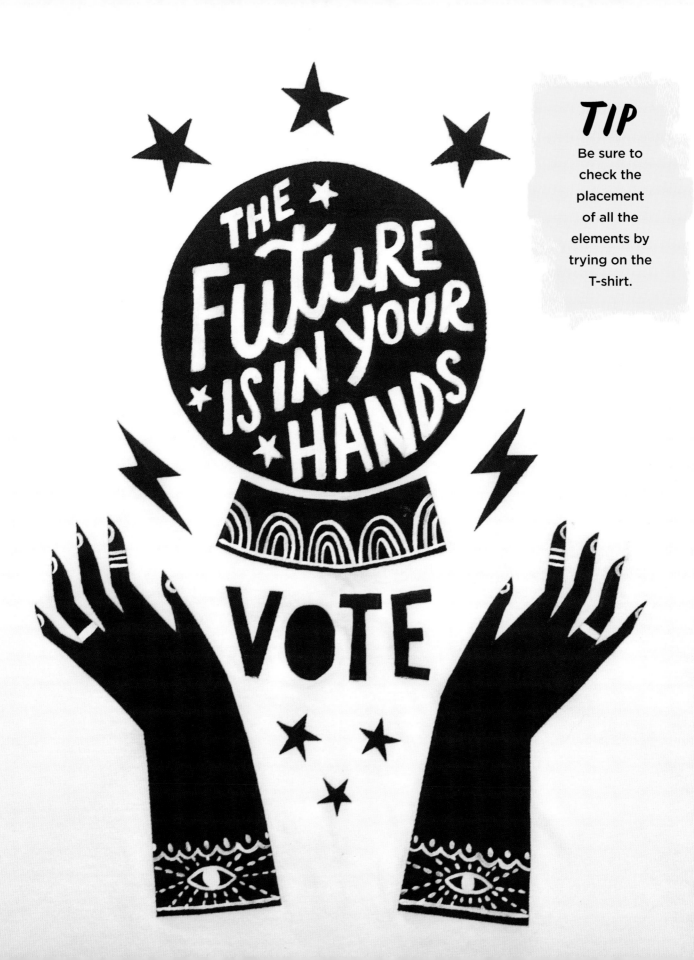

TIP

Be sure to check the placement of all the elements by trying on the T-shirt.

EVENT INVITATION

Fundraising is a great reason to host a party with all of your friends! Make your own simple invitation using markers and Gelly Roll® pens. Pop them in the mail, snap a photo and post it on an event page on social media, or upload it to an e-invitation site like Paperless Post. At your event, set a fundraising goal and ask everyone to pitch in! Remember to include everyone: make cash donations optional and be clear that having fun and raising awareness are your top goals!

WHAT YOU'LL NEED

* At least 2 sheets 8½" x 11" white card stock
* Pencil
* Eraser
* Ruler
* Craft knife
* Cutting mat
* Navy blue and white Sakura Gelly Roll® pens
* Selection of pastel Sakura Koi® brush pens or other markers in pale shades
* Matching A7 envelope(s) (optional)
* Postage stamp(s)

TIPS

Send your invites out at least four weeks in advance, and ask guests to RSVP one to two weeks in advance

✴

Send a text or email reminder the day before

✴

Sell raffle tickets or offer fun games, prizes, and entertainment at your event to raise funds (photo booth, pie-baking contest, game show, free-throw contest)

✴

Ask parents, adults in your community, or local businesses to donate prizes and food

ANDIE BRONSTAD
157 SWELL STREET
SAN DIEGO, CALIF.
9 2 1 2 0

SAVE OUR OCEANS!

PLEASE JOIN US FOR A
POOL PARTY FOR THE
OCEAN CONSERVATORY
APRIL 10TH, 3-5 PM
100 LOMA ST., SAN DIEGO
HOSTED BY AVERY AND CAM
SUGGESTED DONATION $10

R.S.V.P!

THE
OCEAN CONSERVANCY

the ocean conservacy creates
science-based solutions for a
healthy ocean and the wildlife
and communities that depend
on it. THEY'RE AWESOME!

RSVP
www.facebook.com/averysmith

DONATE
www.gofundme.com

1. With a craft knife and ruler, cut down a sheet of card stock to 5″ x 7″. Lightly draw some horizontal guidelines and pencil in your text. When you are happy with the placement, ink over the letters with the blue Gelly Roll® pen.

2. With the brush pens, loosely draw blobs of color for the bodies of fish in various sizes.

3. With the navy blue and white pens, add details and decorative additions to the fish. After everything is completely dry, erase away any pencil marks.

4. For the RSVP card, cut down a piece of card stock to 3½″ x 9¾″ and fold in half. Using the same techniques, decorate the card and add the RSVP information (event page link or contact email/phone) to the inside.

TIP

Use social media or online invitation sites to spread the word and track who's coming!

WILD FEMINIST

STENCILED TOTE BAG

Nigerian writer Chimamanda Ngozi Adichie said it best with her definition of a feminist: a person who believes in the social, political, and economic equality of the sexes. Feminists believe girls and boys should be equally powerful, free, and respected, and that they shouldn't shrink their voices or their ambitions to fit a stereotype. Many feminists also believe that, all things being equal, girls should support each other instead of viewing other girls as competition. So find your voice, use it, and support girls and women leaders who you believe in. Girl power!

WHAT YOU'LL NEED

* Blank tote

* Wild Feminist stencil (page 109)

* Freezer paper

* Pencil

* Scissors

* Craft knife

* Cutting mat

* Iron

* Ironing board

* Neon pink Jacquard® textile paint

* Black Jacquard® textile paint or Black Posca®
  Pen (we used a Posca® Pen)

* Medium size paintbrush

* Small round paintbrush (optional)

INSTRUCTIONS

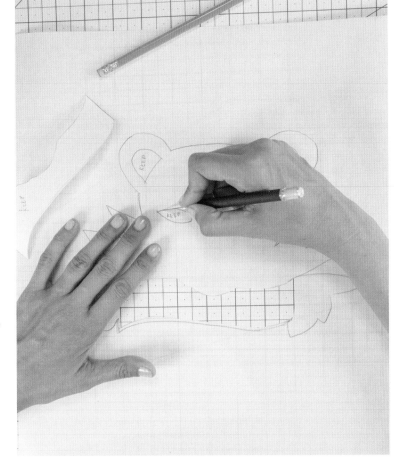

1 Put the Wild Feminist template under a piece of freezer paper (plastic side down) and trace the outline, eyes, inner ear, and inside banner shape with a pencil.

2 Cut out the main shape and set it aside. Cut out the interior ear shapes, eye shapes, and inside banner shape. Discard the rest.

3 Position the main stencil (plastic side down) on the tote, and then place the ears, eyes, and banner. Iron over the stencil (with no steam) until paper is firmly fused to the bag.

4 Paint the exposed areas neon pink and allow to dry completely. Once dry, peel off the freezer paper.

5 With a pencil, lightly draw in the type and details, copying the template. Then ink the details with a black Posca® paint pen or with a small round brush (around size 3 works well) and textile paint.

6 To set the color, iron both sides of the tote with a hot iron for at least 30 seconds at the temperature best suited to the fabric (we used a tea towel between the t-shirt and iron to keep from mucking up the iron). Always wash inside out to prevent fading.

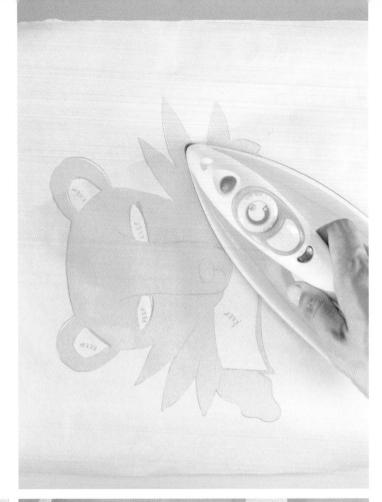

TIP
Freezer paper has a plastic or wax coating on one side, and is an easy way to make any stencil.

WILD FEMINIST

LOVE WINS

BUTTONS

Buttons are an easy, iconic way to express yourself! So go ahead, wear your heart on your sleeve. And if you feel inspired, make a bunch to sell, and donate the proceeds to your favorite charity!

WHAT YOU'LL NEED

* 8½" x 11" sheets of card stock (we used black and white)

* 1½" circle punch or scissors

* 1½" round epoxy stickers

* 1" adhesive pin backs

* Pencil

* Eraser

* Variety of markers, pens, and highlighters (we used a combination of neon Sakura Gelly Roll® pens, highlighters, pastel Sharpie® markers, paint pens, and other markers).

INSTRUCTIONS

1. Punch out or cut out circles from a piece of card stock (or the tear-out buttons on page 111).

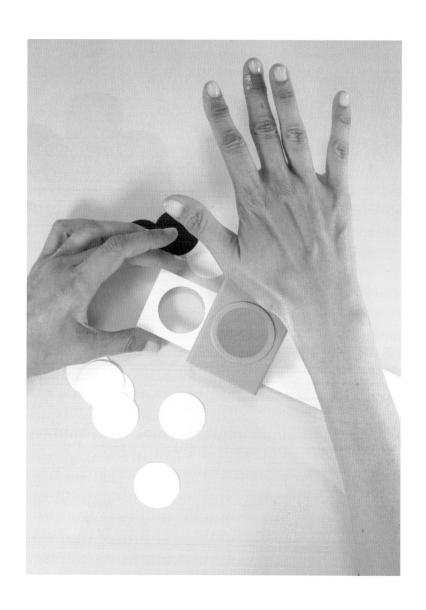

2 Decorate the circles with patterns and your messages. Try different types of pens for different effects. Place a piece of scrap paper under your circle so you can draw patterns that bleed off the edge of the button. For more complicated designs, lightly pencil in the illustration and lettering before writing with markers.

TIP

Use white paint or Gelly Roll® pens on black paper or over other colors to make your message pop!

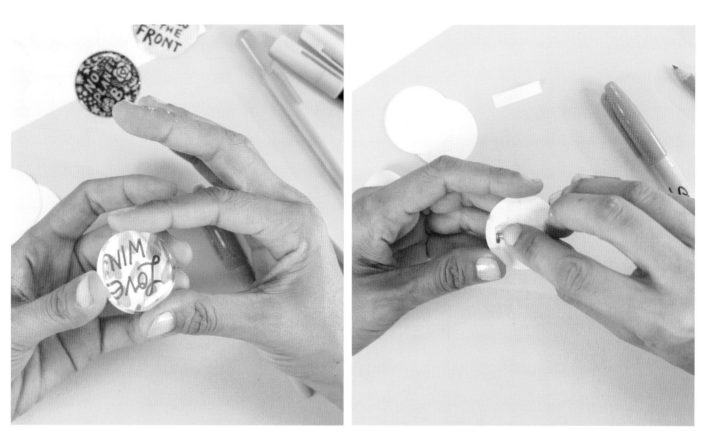

3 Place an epoxy sticker over your decorated circle, and add an adhesive pin back to the back. Be sure to pay attention to the angle of the pin back so your pin is straight.

STAY WOKE

COFFEE MUG

To "Stay Woke" is to stay informed, socially aware, and socially active. It comes from African-American slang (made popular by Erykah Badu's song "Master Teacher") and has been a watchword for the African-American community in challenging the status quo after the 2014 shooting of Michael Brown in Ferguson, Missouri. More recently, it's been taken up by allies and social activists everywhere. Use this mug to make being the change a daily ritual!

WHAT YOU'LL NEED

* Blank coffee mug (we used enamel ware coffee mugs)

* Masking tape

* Pencil

* DecoArt® 1 mm Glass Paint markers in black and pink

* DecoArt® Gloss Enamel in pink (optional)

* Paintbrush (optional)

INSTRUCTIONS

1. Lightly pencil your message and eye pattern onto the mug.

2. Draw in type and pattern with a black glass paint marker. Intersperse a few pink hearts with a glass paint marker or glass enamel. We decorated the handle with stripes.

Other IDEAS

* Speak Up (lips)

* Spread Hope (flowers)

* Rise Up (suns)

* Rise Above (wings)

* Never Give Up (rainbows)

TIP

Try out an alternative design
in different colors!

SWEET CHARITY

LEMONADE STAND

Lemonade stands, bake sales, and car washes are some of the simplest ways to learn how to build a business that gives back. You'll learn business basics like how to provide great customer service and how to earn a profit. Getting customers' attention (a.k.a. marketing) is a key part of any business. That's where creative graphics come in! Use paints and craft paper to create an eye-catching lemonade stand design. Add balloons to give your stand a visual boost, and don't forget to clearly spell out your cause (we chose Kiva International, a nonprofit that lets you and your friends make small loans that change lives to entrepreneurs around the world).

WHAT YOU'LL NEED

* Pencil

* Scissors

* Ruler

* Brown kraft paper roll (wide enough to reach from the top of your table to the ground and wide enough to wrap three sides of the table.)

* Yellow, neon red, and blue tempera paint

* 1½" flat brush (tempera brush will work as well)

* Large round tempera paint brushes

* White & royal blue medium tip Posca® pens

INSTRUCTIONS

 Measure your table and cut a large piece of kraft paper to the length and height of your table. Fold your paper into three sections, two for the sides and one for the front of the table. On the middle section, or the one for the front of the table, sketch out the word "Lemonade" and some strawberries, lemons, and lemon slices.

2 Paint the letters and main fruit shapes with tempera paint. Let dry.

3 Add strawberry and lemon details with blue and white Posca® pens.

4 Use the same techniques to create additional signs and details. We painted an empty cardboard box to highlight our cause and placed our cash jar on top of it.

LEMONADE $1.00
CUPCAKES $2.00

INSPIRED STORY

When she was just four years old, Mikaila Ulmer, with the help of her family, turned her grandma's yummy lemonade recipe and her passion for saving honeybees into Me & the Bees Lemonade! Today, Mikaila is selling her lemonade at Whole Foods and other stores all around the United States. A portion of profits from every bottle go to Heifer International, the Texas Beekeepers Association, and the Sustainable Food Center of Austin, Texas. How sweet is that?!

TIP

Get colorful honeycomb decorations, balloons, cups, and more at shop.ohhappyday.com

STAY BRIGHT!

VINYL LIGHT SWITCH PLATE

Small changes can add up to big impact over time. Consider the energy we use to have lights on, for example. Energy costs money—and causes pollution—so wasting it is not a good idea! You can nudge everyone in your house to save energy with this fun vinyl light switch plate. Stay bright, turn off the lights!

WHAT YOU'LL NEED

* Clear adhesive-backed vinyl (we used glossy)

* Ruler

* Pencil

* Craft knife

* Cutting mat

* Light blue medium point Posca® pen

* Nail polish remover (optional)

* Cotton swabs (optional)

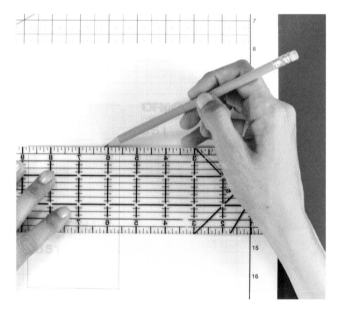

INSTRUCTIONS

1 Measure your switch plate and add ⅛" to each side. Place a sheet of vinyl face down, and draw a rectangle with these measurements in the middle of the sheet. Cut out the rectangle with a craft knife.

> Behavioral scientists refer to a nudge as anything that provides gentle encouragement to make a positive choice. Nudges are smart ways to make change—see if you can think of your own!

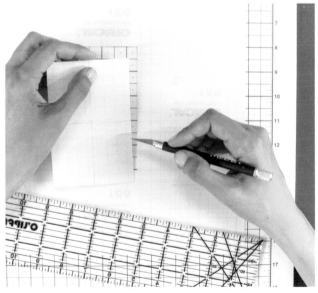

2   Place the vinyl on some scrap paper to protect your work surface. Doodle your illustration around the rectangle with the Posca® pen. If you are not comfortable free-handing, you can first sketch with a pencil, and then go over it with the Posca® pen. If needed, erase any mistakes with nail polish remover and a cotton swab.

3   Cut around your illustration with a pair of scissors, leaving a bit of a white space around the edges.

4   Position the cut out rectangle around the light switch plate. Holding the vinyl in place, peel away 1 or 2 inches of the backing and smooth the vinyl to the wall. Continue to smooth and peel until the entire sticker is in place.

LOUD AND PROUD

PROTEST POSTER

Whether it's a sit-in, sit-down, stand-up, walk-out, or rally, a peaceful protest can be used to build awareness, connection, and community, and can even change laws. Amplify your message by making a creative, handmade sign using simple materials such as cardboard and paint. You can even offer your design to others; we made Hello!Lucky's protest posters for the Women's March on Washington available for download in exchange for a voluntary donation and helped raised thousands of dollars to support the march!

WHAT YOU'LL NEED

* 2 pieces of 18"x 24" cardboard (size optional)

* Pencil

* Craft knife

* Cutting mat

* Blue tempera paint

* Large round paint brush

* Spray paint in neon red, pink, and yellow (we like MTN water-based spray paint because they are low odor)

INSTRUCTIONS

1. Sketch out a pattern of stars, hearts, and abstract shapes on one of your pieces of cardboard and cut out with a craft knife to create your stencil.

2 Cover your work surface with newspaper or other scrap paper to protect it. Place the stencil on top of the second piece of cardboard. This will be your sign. Spray the stencil with stripes of yellow, red, and pink spray paint to create a subtle rainbow effect. Once the paint is dry to the touch, carefully remove the stencil.

3 With a pencil, lightly write out the message. Once you are satisfied with the placement, paint the letters with blue tempera paint, and let dry.

TIPS

If you're organizing your own protest, make sure you get permission from local officials.

*

Get the word out about your event on social media.

*

If there are potential safety issues, report events to the police or other public safety officials.

*

Keep your cool. If someone tries to pick a fight, stay calm and keep safety first.

*

Check out our list of what to bring to a protest on page 43.

SECTION FIVE:

Templates and Tear-Outs

"You can't use up creativity.
The more you use, the more you have."
-Maya Angelou

HOW TO USE THIS SECTION

In the following pages you'll find templates you'll need for the projects on pages 74 and 82.

We've also included postcards, letter-writing sheets, button designs and more that you can tear out and use right away.

HAVE FUN
BEING THE
CHANGE!
THE FUTURE is in
YOUR CAPABLE
HANDS!

VOTE

WILD FEMINIST

 Love WINS

No PLANET B

FEMINIST

GIRLS TO THE FRONT

 PROUD FEMINIST

VOTE

LISTEN UP!

PROTECT OUR OCEANS

No PLANET B

LOVE IS LOVE IS LOVE

SUPPORT PUBLIC SCHOOLS

LOVE IS LOVE

WILD FEMINIST

STOP THE HATE

STAY WOKE

PROTECT OUR PARKS

LOVE IS LOVE IS LOVE

THE FUTURE IS IN YOUR HANDS VOTE

PEACE IS POSSIBLE

SUPPORT PUBLIC SCHOOLS

GIRLS TO THE FRONT

RESCUE IS MY FAVORITE BREED

LOVE SHINES IN DARKNESS

YOU'RE A STAR!

THANKS FOR LENDING A HAND

THANK you

You're the BEST! THANKS!

WE DID IT!

THANK YOU!

LISTEN! ★★★★★ HEAR!

DATE:

DEAR _____,

_____

_____

_____

_____

_____

_____

_____

_____

_____

_____

SINCERELY,

_____

FROM:

SEND TO:

DATE: _____

DEAR _____,

_____

_____

_____

_____

_____

_____

_____

_____

_____

_____

_____

_____

SINCERELY,

_____

FROM:

_____
_____
_____

PLACE
STAMP
HERE

SEND TO:

_____
_____
_____
_____

Use these postcards to get your representative's attention when an issue you care about is up for vote. On the back of the postcard, share a brief personal experience or statistic to support your view, and include your name and address. See page 70 for instructions for making your own postcards!

HELLO.

PLACE
STAMP
HERE

HELLO.

PLACE
STAMP
HERE

Use these postcards to encourage friends, family, and your community to go vote. Color them in, make copies to mail out, and/or post a photo of your card on social media. On the back of the postcard, you can include the election date, a polling place address (if you know it), and information on where they can register to vote. Every vote counts!

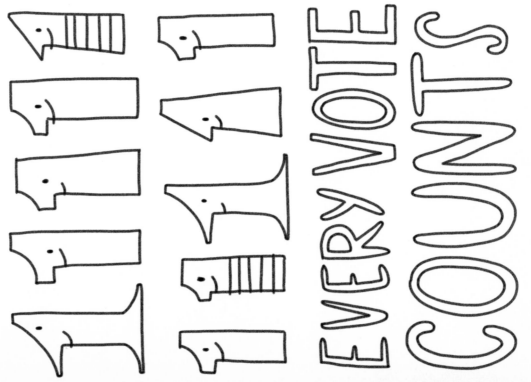

HELLO!

PLACE
STAMP
HERE

....

....

....

....

HELLO!

PLACE
STAMP
HERE↓

....

....

....

....

Use these postcards to connect, inspire, and build momentum for change. On the back of the postcard, jot down an invitation to support a cause or join a community service project, or just say thank you.

PLACE
STAMP
HERE

PLACE
STAMP
HERE

THE WORLD IS A DANGEROUS PLACE NOT BECAUSE OF THOSE WHO DO EVIL BUT BECAUSE OF THOSE WHO LOOK ON AND DO NOTHING.

-ALBERT EINSTEIN

love is love is love

PLACE
STAMP
HERE

_____

_____

_____

_____

PLACE
STAMP
HERE

_____

_____

_____

_____

ACKNOWLEDGMENTS

Thanks to everyone who pitched in to create this book—it truly was a team effort and a real-world example of what it takes to be the change! Alex Bronstad was instrumental in creating this book, as she is in all things Hello!Lucky. We're grateful to Julian Abdey, Sanda Balaban, Joan Blades, Farida Brown, Shana Friedenberg, Marc Kielburger, Cordelia Marchand, Maddie Marchand, Lara Mendel, Erin Murphy, Emma Steadman, and Amy Whitaker for their valuable feedback and encouragement. Props to our wonderful teen models: Shae Ashamalla, Amanda Albrecht, Riley Bream, Andie Bronstad, Haley Buttimer, Ella Burk, Juan Daniel Castrillon-Galvis, Ashley Cortez Chacón, Kira Davirro, Shana Friedenberg, McKenna Gemberling, Paloma Grelier, Lucas Hester, Abby Grant, Talia Hamilton, Hennessy Jones, Elijah Jenkins, Kayla Julio, Taylor Klassen, Jessica Ko, Haley Mack, Alivia Morales, Katie Ohrn, Madai Quevedo, Ivy Roberts-Wright, Martina Shpak, and Abby White. Thank you to theatre director Riley Berris of San Marcos High School who graciously engaged her students in our project, and to McConnell's Fine Ice Cream for allowing us to use their space. Massive thanks to Lara Mendel and The Mosaic Project team, Joan Blades of Living Room Conversations, Pearce Godwin of The Listen First Project, Jamie Gardner, Laura Becker, Arlene Scanlan, Tess Darrow and Kara Yanagawa and the team at Egg Press, and our families for your support and inspiration. Huge thanks to Pauline Molinari, Shelley Baugh, and Julie Chapa at The Quarto Group for your expert guidance. And finally, thanks to our children and to young people everywhere who inspire us every day. Together, we can make a difference!

REFERENCES

AAA Foundation. 2016. "Americans Spend an Average of 17,600 Minutes Driving Each Year." *AAA NewsRoom*, September 6, 2016. newsroom.aaa.com/2016/09/americans-spend-average-17600-minutes-driving-year/.

Arthus-Bertrand, Yann, director. *Human*. Humankind Production, 2015.

Adichie, Chimamanda Ngozi. 2017. "We Should All Be Feminists," Filmed November 2012 at TEDxEuston. Video. www.ted.com/talks/chimamanda_ngozi_adichie_we_should_all_be_feminists.

Csikszentmihalyi, Mihaly. 2009. Flow: *The Psychology of Optimal Experience.* New York: Harper & Row.

Dweck, Carol S. 2017. *Mindset: The New Psychology of Success.* New York: Ballantine Books.

Fiedler, Elizabeth. 2015. "Philadelphia Pizza Lovers Pay It Forward One Slice At A Time." *NPR*, January 14, 2015. www.npr.org/sections/thesalt/2015/01/14/377033772/philadelphia-pizza-lovers-pay-it-forward-one-slice-at-a-time.

Haidt, Jonathan. 2013. *The Righteous Mind: Why Good People are Divided by Politics and Leadership.* New York: Vintage Books.

Hicks, Esther, and Jerry Hicks. 2006. T*he Law of Attraction: The Basics of the Teachings of Abraham.* California: Hay House.

Katie, Byron, and Stephen Mitchell. 2003. *Loving What Is: Four Questions That Can Change Your Life.* New York: Three Rivers Press.

Kielburger, Craig, and Marc Kielburger. 2015. *Me to We: Together We Change the World.* Canada: Me to We.

Kling, Arnold. 2017. *The Three Languages of Politics: Talking Across Political Divides.* Washington, D.C.: Cato Institute.

The Mosaic Project. 2010. *Peacing It Together!: the Mosaic Project's Musical Curriculum & Accompanying Activities.* California: The Mosaic Project.

Pew Research Center. 2017. "U.S. trails most developed countries in voter turnout." May 15, 2017. www.pewresearch.org/fact-tank/2017/05/15/u-s-voter-turnout-trails-most-developed-countries/.

Pew Research Center. 2017. "Millennial and Gen X Voter Turnout Increased in 2016...and Among Millennials, Black Turnout Decreased." May 17, 2017. www.pewresearch.org/fact-tank/2017/05/12/black-voter-turnout-fell-in-2016-even-as-a-record-number-of-americans-cast-ballots/ft_17-05-12_voterturnout_millennialnew/.

Seppala, Emma. 2012. "The Best Kept Secret to Happiness & Health: Compassion." Psychology Today, Sussex Publishers, November 5, 2012. www.psychologytoday.com/blog/feeling-it/201211/the-best-kept-secret-happiness-health-compassion.

United States Department of Agriculture. "U.S. Food Waste Challenge FAQs." USDA Office of the Chief Economist, www.usda.gov/oce/foodwaste/faqs.htm.

Whitaker, Amy. 2016. *Art Thinking: How to Carve Out Creative Space in a World of Schedules, Budgets, and Bosses.* New York: HarperBusiness.

The World Counts. 2017. "People who died from hunger - in the world, this year." www.theworldcounts.com/counters/global_hunger_statistics/how_many_people_die_from_hunger_each_year.